I WANT TO BE . . . Book Series
Creator/Producer: Stephanie Maze of Maze Productions, Inc.
Writer and Educational Consultant: Catherine O'Neill Grace
Designer: Alexandra Littlehales

Photographers for I WANT TO BE AN ENVIRONMENTALIST:
Annie Griffiths Belt, Nicole Bengevino, Scott Goldsmith,
Kevin Monko, Richard Nowitz, Lara Jo Regan,
Joel Sartore, James A. Sugar

Other books available in this series:
I WANT TO BE AN ASTRONAUT
I WANT TO BE A CHEF
I WANT TO BE A DANCER
I WANT TO BE AN ENGINEER
I WANT TO BE A FASHION DESIGNER
I WANT TO BE A FIREFIGHTER
I WANT TO BE A VETERINARIAN

Requests for permission to make copies
of any part of the work should be mailed to:
Permissions Department, Harcourt, Inc.,
6277 Sea Harbor Drive, Orlando, Florida 32887-6777.

Photography credits appear on page 48.

Library of Congress Cataloging-in-Publication Data
Maze, Stephanie.
I want to be an environmentalist/Stephanie Maze;
[writer and educational consultant Catherine O'Neill Grace].
p. cm.—(I want to be—book series)
"A Maze Productions book."
Includes bibliographical references.
Summary: Describes career opportunities within the field of
environmentalism and suggests ways to pursue such a career.
ISBN 0-15-201862-X ISBN 0-15-201939-1 pb
1. Environmental sciences—Vocational guidance—Juvenile literature.
[1. Environmental sciences—Vocational guidance.
2. Vocational guidance] I. Grace, Catherine O'Neill, 1950– .
II. Title. III. Series.
CE80.M39 2000
363.7'0023—dc21 98-52397

First edition
A C E F D B
A C E F D B (pb)

Film processing by A & I Color, Los Angeles
Printed and bound by Tien Wah Press, Singapore

I Want to Be...

AN ENVIRONMENTALIST

A Maze Productions Book

HARCOURT, INC.

SAN DIEGO   NEW YORK   LONDON

ACKNOWLEDGMENTS

We wish to thank the following people, companies, and institutions for their very valuable contributions to this book: U.S. Fish and Wildlife Service; World Wildlife Fund; Conservation International; Sierra Club; John Kermond, Ph.D., National Oceanic and Atmospheric Administration (NOAA), Office of Global Programs; Claudia Nierenberg, NOAA, Office of Global Programs; Cooperative Institute for Research in Environmental Sciences (CIRES)/University of Colorado at Boulder; U.S. Geological Survey; National Science Foundation, Office of Polar Programs; Joseph Goffman, Environmental Defense Fund (EDF); American Red Cross; Earth Conservation Corps; Ohio State University, Department of Environmental Studies; Environmental Studies High School of New York; University of Pennsylvania, Department of Engineering; Brooke Grove Elementary School of Olney, Maryland; Patagonia; Ball Aerospace Systems; CCI Photo Department, NASA Headquarters, Washington, D.C.; Carla Wallace, NOAA Central Library; Institute of Scrap Metal Recycling; Tube City Inc.; U.S. Steel; General Motors; Rachel Carson History Project; Mill Grove Audubon Wildlife Sanctuary; Elite Occasions, Washington, D.C.

Many thanks, also, to all the professionals in this book for allowing us to interrupt their busy schedules and for agreeing to be the wonderful role models children can look up to for many years to come.

To all children who dream the impossible dreams

Where to Start

Do you love to walk in the woods? To explore tidal pools at the seashore? Do animals fascinate you? Are you worried about the pollution of our air and our water?

People who answer yes to questions like these are environmentalists. They care about our planet, Earth. They enjoy its beauty, appreciate its diversity—and want to protect it.

Rachel Carson, a scientist and influential environmentalist, understood why human beings care for their environment. In her 1962 book, *Silent Spring*, she wrote, "Those who contemplate the beauty of the Earth find reserves of strength that will endure as long as life lasts."

As you read this book, you will meet dedicated people who are working hard to protect the many different elements that make up our environment. Some, like the biologist in this picture, monitor wildlife to make sure the animals are healthy. This scientist uses special radio-transmitting equipment to track individual bull walrus among the thousands on a beach in Alaska's Togiak National Wildlife Refuge. Togiak is one of 540 refuges set aside in the United States to provide safe, clean areas for wildlife to breed and rest. Thanks to the efforts of environmentalists at Togiak, spotted seals, walrus, and seven species of whales thrive in the offshore waters.

Types of Environmentalists

Environmentalists work in labs and in the wild, on farms and in offices. In the large photo on the facing page, veterinarians from the U.S. Fish and Wildlife Service and the Florida Department of Natural Resources examine an anesthetized Florida panther. Many Florida panthers used to inhabit swampy areas in the southeastern United States. Today fewer than fifty remain and the Florida panther is considered an endangered species. Habitat loss—the disappearance of land the animals live on, in this case because of development—is a major reason for their decline. Many organizations are working to save this animal.

At top left, Drs. Laura Traci (left) and Margaret Tolbert (right), atmospheric chemists at the Cooperative Institute for Research in Environmental Sciences (CIRES) at the University of Colorado in Boulder, study ice particles in our atmosphere to learn what is causing a hole in Earth's protective ozone layer. Botanist Nalini Nadkarni (left, second from top) examines tree bark in a Costa Rican rainforest. Scientists are anxious to understand rainforests so they can protect those that remain. Professor Roy Stein of Ohio State University and his students (left, second from bottom) check fish in the Olentangy River to determine the wetland's health. Environmental work also goes on in offices, such as the one at left, where lawyers and economists of the Environmental Defense Fund (EDF) map out strategies for protecting the air we breathe.

Chemist

Professor

Botanist

Economist and attorney

Clean air. *In the EDF's Global and Regional Air Program, lawyers Joseph Goffman (center) and Carol Annette Petsonk (right), and economist Sarah Wade (left) discuss possible policies for improving air quality in the United States.*

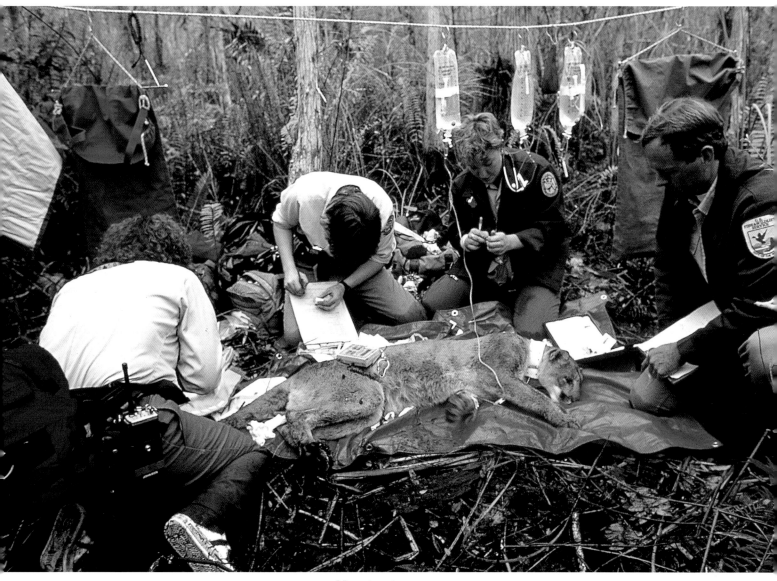

Veterinarian

Organic farmer

Biologist

Chemical matters. *At One Straw Farm in White Hall, Maryland, the Drew Norman family grows produce organically without using pesticides and chemicals that can potentially harm humans and the environment (above left). Biologist John Harte (above right), a professor at the University of California, Berkeley, studies the effects of acid rain (see page 20).*

Loss of resources

Loss of species

Too darn hot. *This color-enhanced photograph highlights the gases emitted by a factory in Alberta, Canada. Around the world, the burning of fuel by factories and other sources contributes to a problem called global warming, a gradual increase in Earth's temperature caused by the buildup of carbon dioxide and other gases. These gases prevent heat given off by Earth from escaping into space. The warming may be changing Earth's climates and oceans.*

Global warming

Air pollution

Water pollution

Eco-Issues

Human activity, such as building cities, manufacturing goods, and driving cars, has put our planet's delicate systems in danger, especially during the past century. Forests, resources that help produce oxygen to support life on Earth and shelter many animals, are in danger of disappearing as people cut down trees for lumber (facing page, top left) and burn rainforests to create farm fields (facing page, top right). Wetlands are swallowed up by housing developments (top right). Factory emissions affect the chemical balance of the atmosphere, causing acid rain. Fertilizer runoff from farm fields disrupts the life cycles of fish and water plants. Oil spills, such as the *Exxon Valdez's* 1989 accident in Alaska, contaminate water and kill animals (facing page, bottom right). Poaching for valuable furs has driven some wildlife to near extinction (inset picture, above). Earth's growing population is also an environmental issue. Large numbers of people competing for space put strain on the land and its limited natural resources. Where people, and their vehicles and factories, crowd together, air pollution can result (facing page, bottom left). Environmentalists think about how to address these problems. If you decide to be an environmentalist, you can help find solutions.

Habitat loss

Population increase

Urban sprawl. *Mexico City, Mexico (above), has a population of more than twenty million, making it the largest city on Earth. Here, as in a number of other major cities around the world, the huge population has led to many problems, such as severe air pollution.*

Waste Renewal: Recycling Scrap Metal

Human activity produces piles of waste—including metal. But many metals such as steel, used to manufacture all kinds of useful objects—from cars to suspension bridges to cans—are 100 percent recyclable. This means that the metal that forms an old school bus, an aluminum can, or a rusty car frame can be reclaimed and reused instead of taking up precious space in a garbage dump.

Iron and steel are currently the most recycled materials in the United States. Recycling iron and steel saves money, ore (the minerals from which metal is made), and energy—and the savings are big! The Environmental Protection Agency (EPA) estimates that recycling scrap iron and steel instead of making new materials results in a 74 percent savings in energy and an 86 percent reduction in air pollution.

The photographs on these pages, all taken in Pittsburgh, Pennsylvania, show how scrap metal is recycled. In the large photo above, a giant crane at Tube City, a scrap-metal processing

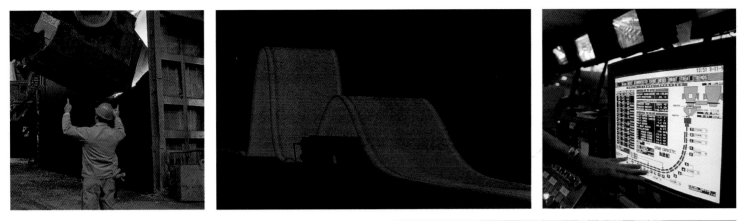

plant, carries a car to a feeder belt that leads to a shredder. At the shredder, the car and other scrap are pulverized into small pieces. Cans from recycling programs are baled into bundles (inset photo, facing page).

From Tube City, bundles of steel are transported by rail or truck to the steel mill at Edgar Thomson Works, part of U.S. Steel. There, under supervision of a steelworker, they are mixed with molten iron in a high-temperature furnace and converted to molten steel (top left). The molten steel is then poured into a caster that shapes it into red-hot slabs of useful steel. A computer-aided manufacturing system (CAM) helps manage the process (top right). The hot slabs are flattened into sheets (top center) and rolled into coils as tall as people (right, second from top).

The scrap-metal recycling system provides about half of the iron, steel, copper, and lead, and a third of the aluminum used in American factories.

In 1997 enough steel was reclaimed from old automobiles to produce almost thirteen million new ones. Remember that old car you saw being picked up by a crane? The metal it was made of was recycled and came back as a brand-new car!

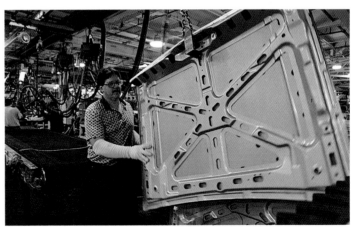

Old is new. *At Fisher Body Works, part of General Motors in Pittsburgh, Pennsylvania, autoworkers use recycled steel to build strong, safe parts for new vehicles. Here workers move the hood of a truck (above) and inspect a car door (right).*

Hands-on science. *At the Smithsonian Environmental Research Center, students from a Maryland elementary school explore aspects of a great American environmental treasure: the Chesapeake Bay.*

Education

There are hundreds of environmental education programs designed for kids going on right now all over the United States—at museums, nature centers, schools, and national and state parks. If you're interested in getting involved in environmental work, signing up for one of these programs would be a great place to start.

Environmental education programs often offer the chance to step right into real research projects. That's what the students from Brooke Grove Elementary School in Olney, Maryland, got to do when they took a field trip to the Smithsonian Environmental Research Center (SERC) on Chesapeake Bay in Edgewater, Maryland. The students visited several research stations set up along the Rhode River, a tidal stream that empties into the Chesapeake. They measured water quality (facing page, top left), studied oyster beds and their habitat with a microscope (facing page, top right), and found out all about the life cycle of crabs (large photo, left). Lessons at SERC are led by working environmental scientists who are engaged in ongoing research at the Chesapeake Bay site.

The SERC education program is designed to teach kids about the Chesapeake Bay's ecosystems (see page 20), as well as about global environmental issues. The center, like other environmental education sites and programs, hopes to provide young people with the knowledge, skills, and tools they need to become responsible citizens of our planet.

A closer look. *Environmental science can include the study of both the natural world and high technology. At top, middle school students examine an alligator skin at a workshop conducted by the U.S. Fish and Wildlife Service. Above, students at the University of Pennsylvania's mechanical engineering department work on their senior project: designing a solar-powered car that runs on energy captured from the sun's rays instead of gasoline, saving energy and reducing pollution.*

15

High School for Environmental Studies

New York City might seem like an unusual place to study the natural world. But that's just what the students shown on these pages from the High School for Environmental Studies (HSES) are doing. In the large photo above, Zenia Del Gado tends basil plants that she and her classmates are raising for their botany class. They're studying hydroponics, the science of growing plants in water and liquid nutrients rather than soil. At left, another student waters the school's rooftop garden.

HSES is a New York City public school. Its eight hundred students take typical classes, from language arts and math to science and phys ed. But the school's primary goal is to "promote an environmentally conscious citizenry." HSES was founded, in part, because educators believe that there will be many career opportunities in environmentalism in the twenty-first century.

Specialized classes include environmental law, environmental health, wildlife conservation, and various science courses. In social studies, students compare and contrast natural and man-made environments. At right center, Lyonell Edmonds feeds the fish in his marine biology classroom. Concern for the planet is also at the center of many extracurricular activities. At top right, members of the student recycling team sort into bins paper, soda cans, and other trash. At the end of the school day, the team goes to each classroom to collect used materials and dispose of them appropriately. School events also have an environmental theme. For graduation 1998, the gym became a rainforest. At bottom right, Jeff Cole works on a mural depicting tropical trees.

Nature up close. *Juniors and seniors from HSES help out at Nature Day in Central Park, an event organized by The Nature Conservancy. The students guide younger kids from around the city through "eco-tents" that display live plants and animals. Above, visitors check out a small alligator—carefully!*

Other Programs

The kids on these pages are involved in a wide range of environmental activities that are fun *and* educational. Each year in order to breed, Pacific salmon swim upstream from the ocean to the waters where they were hatched. But often they find their original habitats have changed. Logging and pollution have damaged the streams where the salmon lay their eggs, and dams and dikes built on rivers can prevent fish from even completing their journey. But there is hope! In the inset photo above, Native American student volunteers release baby salmon into a stream in Oregon—part of the Salmon Restoration Project of the Earth Conservation Corps—bypassing a barrier that would have kept the fish from completing their migration. Community recycling programs like the one in Tucson, Arizona (below left), are another great way for kids to help improve the environment. Learning about organic farming at a place such as Emandal, a farm in Willits, California, can help, too (below right). Zoos and museums are also good places to learn about the earth. At the Amazonia exhibit at the National Zoo in Washington, D.C., visitors find out what it's like to walk in a rainforest (facing page, bottom left). At the Boston Museum of Science, they learn about climate (facing page, bottom right).

Hello there! Swimmer Steven Clever visits the Dolphin Quest Learning Center in Hawaii (below). Underwater, Steven can hear clicking sounds that are sonar signals dolphins make to navigate as well as to locate objects. Educational programs likes this one offer human beings a rare chance to interact with and understand sea animals.

Environmental Vocabulary

While the word *environmentalist* once identified a kind of scientist, today it also represents a way of life and a way of thinking. The terms on these pages were once heard only in laboratories, but they are now common in conversations at rallies, in classrooms, and around some families' dinner tables.

ACID RAIN

When sulfuric acid and nitric acid emitted by the smokestacks of factories that burn coal and oil combine with water in the atmosphere, acid rain, fog, or snow forms. Weather patterns carry the acid rain over broad areas, often far from the factories that created the pollution. Acid rain damages trees and other plants, as well as buildings. It also affects the natural balance of lakes and rivers, and harms the fish, plants, and amphibians that live in them.

ECOSYSTEM

An ecosystem is a community of plants and animals that interact with each other and their physical environment. All parts of an ecosystem are interdependent. The ecosystem shown here is a wetland in the Mississippi Delta that is home to flocks of white pelicans. American wetlands provide habitat for hundreds of bird and fish species, but many of these ecosystems are threatened by construction projects.

OZONE LAYER

The ozone layer consists of an invisible gas that surrounds the planet about twelve miles above sea level. The layer protects the earth from damaging radiation from the sun. Scientists are concerned about the development of a hole in the ozone layer. The hole, which lies above Antarctica, is colored pink in this satellite picture. Experts believe the hole is the result of manmade pollutants called chlorofluorocarbons (CFCs).

REMOTE OPERATING VEHICLE

The National Oceanic and Atmospheric Administration (NOAA) uses vehicles like this to conduct research on the deep ocean, where humans cannot go. This research provides data about changes in the ocean's temperature, volume, and chemical composition. Oceans cover about 70 percent of Earth's surface, yet scientists are only beginning to understand the oceans' complex systems and their role in maintaining life.

SEINE NET

First used for hauling in schools of fish, seine (pronounced *sayn*) nets were targeted by activists because dolphins were unnecessarily trapped and killed in the nets. Fishermen now use redesigned nets that allow dolphins to escape. Researchers still rely on seine nets to capture a variety of species in a study area.

HYDROLAB

The U.S. Fish and Wildlife Service uses a Hydrolab here to monitor water quality. The sophisticated, automatic equipment allows scientists to track from a distance many aspects of water quality. Hydrolabs are used in fresh- and saltwater environments, where even subtle changes can affect plant and animal life. They're useful for analyzing pollutants in groundwater and wastewater.

COMPOSTING

This method for disposing of garden and household waste mirrors the decomposition that occurs in nature. Leaves and other waste are layered with soil, then dampened to start the process. Sometimes worms are added to speed decomposition. The nutrient-rich compost makes excellent fertilizer. Composting is an important part of organic farming.

PARABOLIC MICROPHONE

Wildlife biologists use a variety of high-tech equipment to track animals in their natural environment. One of the challenges of the work is to observe animals without disturbing them. This parabolic microphone allows a researcher to locate and record sounds from a great distance. It is especially useful for studying birds and other flying creatures such as bats.

SPECTROMETER

A spectrometer measures the activity of tiny bits of matter: atomic particles and chemical elements. Analyzing them allows scientists to understand the building blocks of life-forms and natural systems. This technician is using the equipment to analyze information about the chemical composition of Earth's protective ozone layer.

WEATHER SATELLITE

The study of global weather patterns is important to many environmentalists. The data reveal changing temperature patterns that may indicate global warming. They help predict storms and show scientists how human activity affects natural systems. This weather satellite will gather billions of pieces of data about Earth's weather and climate.

History of Environmentalism

*Early observers.
Above, from left:
Thales of Miletus
wrote about the
connection of
water and life;
Pliny the Elder, a
Roman, observed
the eruption of the
volcano Vesuvius;
Avicenna, an
Arab scientist,
studied fossils.*

Innovators. *Below, from left: Alexander von Humboldt was a naturalist; Thomas Malthus studied population growth; Charles Darwin developed the theory of evolution.*

Although the environmental movement as we know it began in the twentieth century, humans have been trying to understand our relationship with the environment for thousands of years. As far back as 500 B.C., the great philosopher Aristotle knew that deforestation causes erosion, now recognized as an environmental problem. Italian Giovanni Boccaccio (second row from bottom, far left) was one of the first to study population, documenting the great plague of the Middle Ages that greatly reduced Europe's population. As scientific observations and technology became more sophisticated, so did human understanding. But sometimes new problems were created. The horse collar and plow of the Middle Ages (left, second from top) changed forever the way land was cultivated—increasing, for example, the speed at which farmers cut down forests to make way for fields. Christopher Columbus's voyage to the New World eventually led to massive human migrations, which disrupted most Native Americans' harmonious relationship to the land (left, third from top). The invention of the microscope allowed scientists such as Antony van Leeuwenhoek (second row from bottom, right) to analyze the tiniest microorganisms and laid the foundation for understanding our world better.

The Industrial Revolution of the late eighteenth century brought great technological advances—and a new set of problems. The use of natural resources, such as coal, increased.

Visionaries. Physicist Julius Robert von Mayer (far left) studied energy. Henry David Thoreau (left, center) endorsed harmony with nature.

Factory smokestacks and, eventually, automobiles began polluting air and water. People slowly started to understand that the earth needed protection.

Environmental legislation in the United States dates to the late nineteenth century, when President Abraham Lincoln signed a law protecting Yosemite Valley from loggers. Yellowstone, the first national park (top right), was created in 1872. In the early 1900s the government began to set aside more land for parks and wildlife refuges, led by President Theodore Roosevelt and naturalist John Muir (top, third from left). In 1916 the National Park Service was created to manage America's growing park system. But it wasn't until the 1950s and 1960s that the environmental movement as we know it took off. In 1962 scientist Rachel Carson (second from top, left) opened many people's eyes with her book *Silent Spring,* which imagined a frightful future for the world if pesticide use, such as crop dusting (second from top, right) continued without controls. Earth Day was observed for the first time on April 22, 1970. Organizers expected a crowd—but were shocked when twenty million people celebrated around the country in gatherings like this one in New York (third from bottom)!

Worth saving. *A moose stands in a lake in Denali National Park, Alaska (above). To protect the earth, researchers at Ball Aerospace Systems ready a research satellite (right).*

High Tech

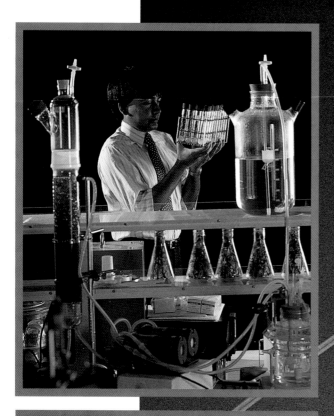

The high-tech research projects on these pages are designed to address a huge array of environmental problems, including world hunger, air and water pollution, and the depletion of the ozone layer. Here, researchers from McMurdo Station in Antarctica prepare to launch a balloon that will rise about twelve miles above Earth to gather data about the ozone layer. The project is a joint venture of the National Oceanic and Atmospheric Administration (NOAA) and the Cooperative Institute for Research in Environmental Sciences (CIRES) at the University of Colorado in Boulder. NOAA and CIRES scientists work together to describe, monitor, and predict changes in the earth's environment. Cooperative research projects like this one in Antarctica are an important part of that work.

At top left, a researcher at Escagenetics, a biotechnology company in San Carlos, California, works on developing new kinds of food. Crops that are

created in controlled environments, such as laboratories, or that are resistant to pests so they don't need chemical sprays can have less impact on the planet—and can help alleviate world hunger. At far left, center, a meteorologist monitors strikes at the lightning detection center at the National Severe Storms Laboratory in Norman, Oklahoma. At far left, bottom, a computer-controlled irrigation system brings water to the Negev Desert, in Israel, creating fertile soil for crops, which help feed growing populations. Underwater exploration equipment allows a NOAA researcher to explore the ocean depths (top right), and collect samples for analysis. CIRES scientists study the makeup of chlorofluorocarbons (CFCs), gases that are damaging the ozone layer (right center). Engineering students at the University of California, Davis, sit in an environmentally friendly hybrid car that runs on electricity but can switch over to gasoline (right).

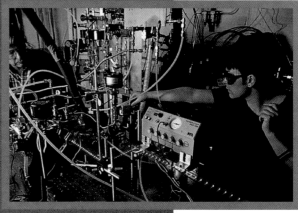

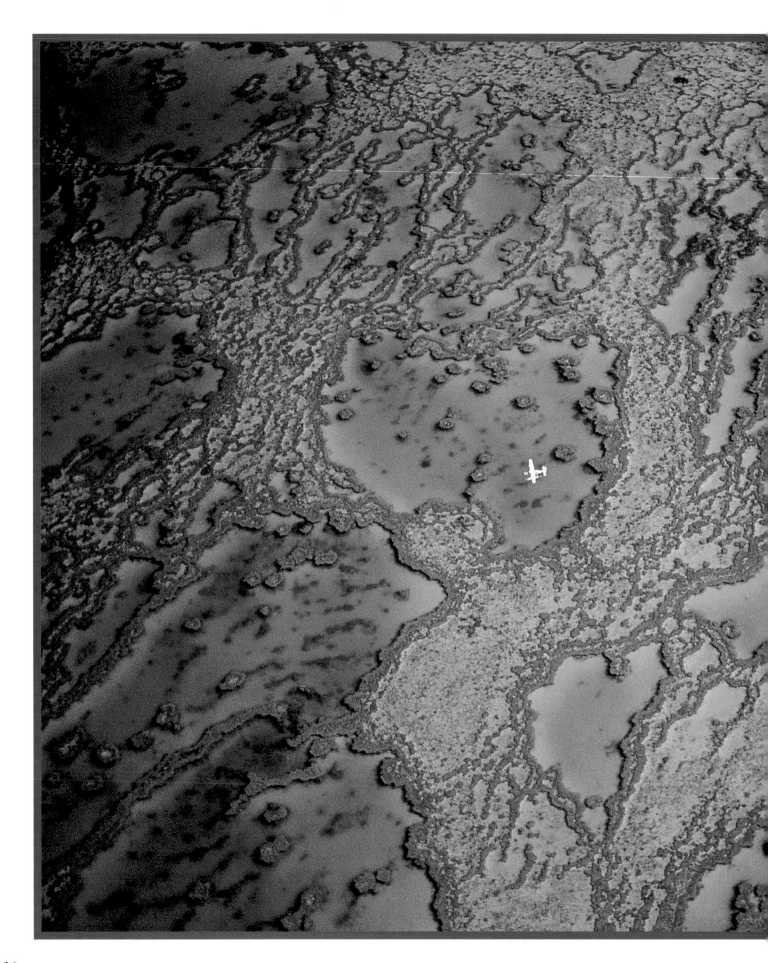

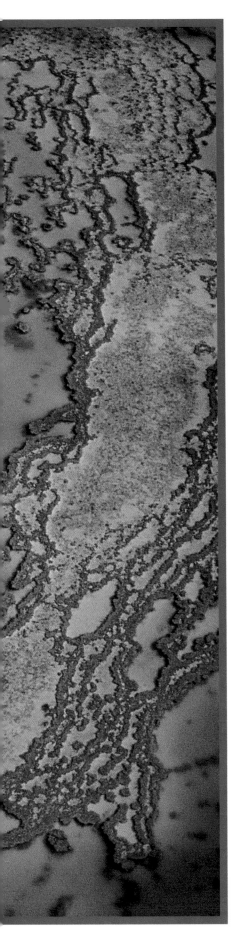

Did You Know . . .

. . . that Australia's Great Barrier Reef (left), the largest coral reef in the world, is an amazing example of biodiversity—Earth's vast array of life forms. The reef stretches for 1,250 miles and shelters more than 1,500 types of fish, 4,000 species of mollusks, and 500 kinds of seaweed. In some places it is more than four hundred feet thick.

. . . that in the year 2,000 B.C. the population of the earth was probably only four million. Between 1950 and 1998, the world's population more than doubled to nearly 6 billion, and it is projected to reach almost 12.5 billion by A.D. 2050 according to the United Nations!

. . . that tropical forestland shrinks by about eighty thousand square miles each year due to expanding agriculture, logging, and development? It is estimated that one square mile of rainforest is destroyed every six minutes. Environmentalists are working to save remaining forests, which shelter the widest variety of animals and plants found anywhere, including plants that provide 25% of all medicines in the world.

. . . that 55 percent of air pollution in the United States is caused by sources of transportation, such as cars, trucks, buses, and planes?

. . . that hot water from natural geysers is used to heat homes and offices in Reykjavík, the capital of Iceland, an island nation with many volcanoes?

. . . that in a typical year scrap-metal recyclers in the United States handle some fifty-five million tons of scrap iron and steel—enough to build seven thousand Eiffel Towers!

. . . that in Saudi Arabia there are solar-powered pay phones in the desert?

. . . that recycling a ton of paper saves seventeen trees?

. . . that the oceans of the world cover an area that is thirty-seven times the size of the United States?

El Niño

Within a day, the weather can change quickly. Think of how a summer thunderstorm can transform a sunny hot day into a dark and blustery one in less than an hour.

Earth's climate—the average weather from year to year—changes, too. Many factors interact to create climate—from the currents in the atmosphere and in the oceans to the temperature of the land.

The oceans have a large capacity to store and release heat, which affects global climate profoundly. Sometimes the surface temperature of the tropical Pacific Ocean warms up, creating unusual weather events all over the world. The scientific name for this effect is the Southern Oscillation, but most people know it as El Niño. El Niño means "the boy" (or "the Christ child") in Spanish. The name was adopted because of the weather pattern's tendency to be at full force

28

around Christmas. The effects of El Niño last as long as eighteen months and can cause destructive weather, from droughts to flooding.

These pictures illustrate El Niño–related weather events worldwide in recent years. In 1997 El Niño contributed to drought in Zaire, Africa (facing page, inset); tornadoes such as the one in Spencer, South Dakota (facing page, large photo); hurricanes in Wilmington, North Carolina (above left); and heavy snow in Portland, Oregon (above center). The effect brought a warmer winter in Canada, a scorching summer in the southern United States, wildfires in Borneo, and smaller than usual harvests in Brazil.

An opposite cooling weather trend called La Niña ("the girl") occurs after some, but not all, El Niños. This pattern also affects global climate, causing effects such as an increased frequency of Atlantic Ocean hurricanes, brutal winters in Canada, and torrential rain in Southeast Asia.

Scientists are concerned because, since 1976, the El Niño effect seems to be on the rise. Global warming caused by the buildup of gases in the atmosphere that keep heat from escaping into outer space may be a factor. Maybe someday you will join the effort to understand El Niño.

World of water. Floodwater fills the streets of St. Louis, Missouri (above right). The 1997–98 El Niño was the strongest recorded in this century. It pushed temperature and precipitation to record levels in many places.

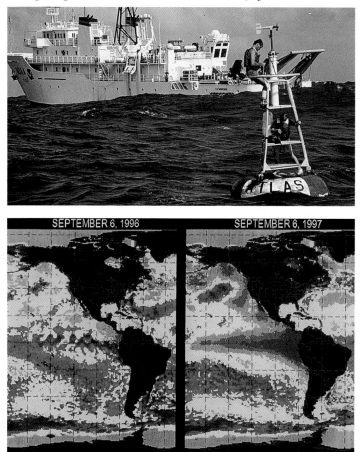

NOAA knows. *The NOAA ship* Ka'imimoana *(above center) services a mooring that collects data on El Niño patterns. This data is beamed up to a satellite and back to Earth. Images such as the one above showing temperature changes from 1996-1997 can then be accessed via the Internet from anywhere on Earth.*

Endangered Species

An endangered species is a particular kind of plant or animal that may die out, or become extinct, because of habitat loss, overfishing, or hunting. Once a species is extinct, it is lost forever. These examples are only a few of more than fifteen hundred endangered species that environmentalists hope to save.

HESPEROMANNIA LYDGATEI

CHAPMAN RHODODENDRON

DUDLEYA TRASKIAE

MAHOE

GREEN PITCHER PLANT

PYGMY FRINGE TREE

ROUND-LEAF BIRCH

LANGE METALMARK

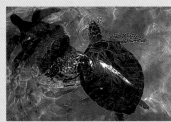
GREEN SEA TURTLE

SNAIL DARTER

LEAST BELL VIREO

YACARÉ CAIMAN

PEREGRINE FALCON

ATLANTIC SALT MARSH SNAKE

GALAPAGOS TORTOISE

MANATEE

BLACK-FOOTED FERRET

MONTE VERDE TOAD

ATTWATER PRAIRIE CHICKEN

BROWN PELICAN

SPOTTED OWL

ORANGUTAN

CALIFORNIA CONDOR

SIBERIAN TIGER

MADAGASCAR LEMUR

PANDA

BACTRIAN CAMEL

GREVY ZEBRA

THIN-SPINED PORCUPINE

AFRICAN BLACK RHINOCEROS

HUMPBACK WHALE

SNOW LEOPARD

AFRICAN ELEPHANT

CHEETAH

FLORIDA PANTHER

GRIZZLY BEAR

GRAY WOLF

JAGUAR

Return of the Eagle

The bald eagle has been a symbol of the United States since the Revolutionary War. But by the early 1970s the eagles had begun to disappear. Hunting the huge eagles—which have wingspans of six feet or more—was made illegal in 1940, but many were still being killed. Others died out because their habitats had been destroyed; still others fell prey to poisoning by a pesticide, DDT, which was banned in 1972. A population once numbering fifty thousand had dwindled to only eight hundred breeding pairs in the lower forty-eight states.

In 1983 a campaign to save the eagle was mounted. The pictures on these pages were taken at the George Miksch Sutton Avian Research Center in Bartlesville, Oklahoma, where biologists worked during the 1980s and early 1990s to encourage the growth of the eagle population. The Sutton Center was one of several eagle recovery stations throughout the country.

Above, Wayne Norton retrieves an eagle egg from a nest in a seventy-five-foot-tall pine tree in Florida. The egg will be carefully packed (inset photo, left) and flown to the Sutton Center in an airplane. There it will incubate and hatch. Below left, biologists drape camouflage jackets over their faces to keep baby eaglets from seeing them. The researchers don't want the eagles to associate humans with food, which might keep them from hunting on their own when they're released. Humans raise the eaglets until they are ready to fly and hunt in the wild. At bottom right, Sutton Center director Steve Sherrod holds a bald eagle as assistant director M. Alan Jenkins attaches a U.S. Fish and Wildlife Service band to its leg so they can identify the bird later if it is injured or killed. The bird, raised in captivity, is about to be released into the wild.

In the 1980s and 1990s, the bald eagle made a steady recovery because of programs like the one at the Sutton Center. The growth in population has been so impressive that the bald eagle is no longer considered an endangered species.

These pictures were taken in 1992, just before the Sutton program ended. The eaglets you see here are probably flying free somewhere in the United States right now. Our national symbol is on the wing once more!

Time to hatch. *An eaglet is gently released from its shell (left). After researchers removed this egg from its nest, to incubate and hatch in the lab, the mother laid new eggs to replace it.*

Babying a bird. *Technician Tracie Darnell uses a puppet to feed a day-old chick (above). The hand puppet ensures that the eaglet identifies with its own species, not humans. When this chick grows up, it will be released into the wild.*

33

Some Alternative Solutions

One of the most important jobs that environmental scientists do is to develop alternative ways to generate energy and encourage environmentally friendly lifestyles. The world's supply of oil, coal, and gas will run out eventually—but human beings will still require heat and light and power to survive. And even while these fossil fuels are still available, they produce pollution when they are burned. Alternative energy sources are a necessity!

The background photograph on these pages shows turbines on a wind farm in Tehachapi, California. Wind farms in California generate about 1 percent of the state's energy needs—and this clean source has the potential to provide much more. Other alternative methods for creating electrical power include harnessing the sun's energy through solar-panel technology (facing page, top) and burning tires (facing page, bottom left) to run turbines in a power plant that supplies more than three thousand homes in Wesley, California. Special scrubbers remove pollutants from the smoke the tires create as they burn.

The way people choose to live their lives can make a difference in the environment, too. Below left, a healer treats a patient with an alternative therapy using sound and massage. The house below at right, called The Castle, takes recycling to a grand scale—it was built from used tires and aluminum cans!

Plastic, please. Millions of pounds of plastic are thrown away every year to accumulate in landfills. Plastics take centuries to fully decompose, but biologists have discovered a method to make biodegradable plastics using plant material (near left).

NOW MORE THAN EVER ... SAVE THE BAY!

CAUTION LIQUID IN GLASS

CAUTION
EYE PROTECTION MUST BE WORN IN THIS AREA

LIQUID IN GLASS

LIQUID IN GLASS

Using caution. *Disposing of toxic waste responsibly is a necessity to protect the environment. At near left, a worker wears protective gear and a ventilating mask while handling poisonous pollutants.*

Related Professions

There are a wide variety of career paths that lead into the field of environmentalism. In the large photo, a U.S. Fish and Wildlife scuba diver carries a special underwater clipboard to take notes as he studies plants and animals in Rose Atoll in Hawaii and thinks about how to protect them.

Environmental activists remind people and the government of the dangers of pollution and other threats to our ecosystems. A woman uses a sign (facing page, bottom left) to draw attention to the need to protect the Chesapeake Bay from dangers such as fertilizer runoff and overfishing of crabs and other creatures.

U.S. Fish and Wildlife Service workers are government employees who serve in a wide variety of jobs to help the agency fulfill its mission to protect our nation's living creatures. Some work with animals in the wild. A wildlife veterinarian carries an anesthetized wolf (top left) as part of a relocation of the gray wolf from Canada to the American West. An ichthyologist, or fish specialist, removes eggs from an Atlantic salmon in a program to help the population grow larger (bottom left). Others work with chemicals. At left center, a technician examines waste for pollution.

Whatever you'd like to pursue—from writing slogans to raising salmon—you can find a way to do it as an environmentalist.

You Can Make a Difference

Food from the 'Hood. *After riots rocked Los Angeles in 1992, high school kids in the affected neighborhoods wanted to do something for the community. So they reclaimed a weedy unused lot and planted a community garden with flowers, lettuce, collards, and other vegetables. Some of the produce they grow goes to needy families; the rest is sold at farmers' markets. The group sells salad dressing, too. The success of Food from the 'Hood proves that kids can make a difference!*

Environmental problems aren't limited to such overwhelming disasters as oil spills, toxic waste, or rainforest destruction. Some other problems can be addressed—and corrected—by everyday action taken by ordinary people, including kids. Here are some things that you, your friends, and your family can try doing to help our planet:

• Buy "green" products—food and other goods that have less environmental impact than regular products because they use few artificial colors, come in recycled and/or biodegradable packaging, and are made from recycled materials.

• Use the microwave more often than the oven for cooking. A microwave cooks faster and uses less energy.

• Turn off your computer at night and on weekends to conserve energy.

• Clean your lightbulbs. Dirty ones can reduce light by up to 25 percent and use up more electricity.

• When you go to the beach, pick up any litter you see and dispose of it to keep it out of the water. Cut up any plastic six-pack rings before you throw them away. Left uncut the rings can choke fish or seabirds.

• In the winter keep the heat as low as you comfortably can. If you're chilly, exercise or put on a sweater!

• Use compact fluorescent bulbs instead of regular bulbs. They last ten times longer and use 25 percent less energy.

• Plant a tree. A tree provides shade, shelters animals and birds, and produces oxygen for all animals to breathe.

Recycling works! *Did you know that Americans throw out twenty-eight billion bottles every year? And that we use eighty billion aluminum soda cans? These young people in Long Beach, California, started a squad to collect and properly dispose of recyclable materials. Here they are resting after picking up and bagging bottles and other material from a riverside. You and your friends could start a recycling squad in your neighborhood.*

• When you go shopping, use a cloth sack to carry what you buy. A cloth sack reduces excessive waste produced by paper and plastic bags.

• Walk or bike to school or work, to reduce air pollution—and to increase your physical fitness! If you live too far away to walk, start a carpool or use public transportation.

• Celebrate Christmas with a live tree and plant it in your yard when the holiday is over.

• Keep a cloth towel by the kitchen sink and use it instead of a handful of paper ones.

• If you take your lunch to school, pack it in reusable plastic containers. Use a lunch box instead of a paper sack to carry it in.

• Give away magazines and books you no longer want. Libraries, schools, or nursing homes would be glad to have them.

• Start a compost heap to recycle garbage and create fertilizer for your garden.

• Turn off the faucet when you're brushing your teeth. This saves gallons of water!

• Give your holiday gifts in reusable bags or tins. Wrap packages in a cloth or scarf instead of paper. If you want to use wrapping paper, reuse it, recycle it, or make your own.

• Give memberships in or donations to conservation organizations as gifts.

• Put up a bird feeder. Keep a list of the types of birds it attracts.

• Start an environmental club at school or in your neighborhood.

• Run the dishwasher and washing machine only when they're full.

• Choose a career as an environmentalist!

Global Efforts

People throughout the world are involved in environmental efforts to protect animals and plants, reduce pollution, and save natural areas. In the large picture at right, a wildlife worker in China cradles an orphaned Siberian tiger cub. The world's largest cat, the Siberian tiger is also one of the most endangered. Its range has been reduced to a few isolated pockets of land. Because of habitat loss and poaching for their skins, fewer than two hundred of the great cats now survive in the wild. But international cooperation offers hope for the Siberian tiger. With the help of the World Wildlife Fund, the Tiger Trust in Britain, and the University of Idaho's Hornocker Wildlife Research Institute, Siberian tiger preservation sites are being created and research is being done to help save this beautiful animal. This project is one of hundreds that the World Wildlife Fund supports all over the planet.

Preserving energy resources is also a pressing issue worldwide. Brazil and many other countries are working to find alternatives to limited fossil fuels. At top left on the facing page, huge vats of sugarcane juice ferment in São Paulo, Brazil. The material will be processed into ethanol, a clean-burning alcohol, which many Brazilians use as fuel. As the world's largest producer of sugar, Brazil developed an efficient way of making ethanol from sugarcane. Today sixteen billion liters are produced annually. Not only is ethanol less polluting than gasoline, it is also made from a renewable resource.

Helping hands. *Dr. Dagmar Werner of the World Wildlife Fund studies iguanas (top). A scientist analyzes algae in Germany, a country at the forefront of the environmental movement (center). Marine biologist Dr. Sylvia Earle examines coral in the Australian Great Barrier Reef (above).*

Mapping the forests.
At the Tropical Forest Technical Center in Vincennes, France, a cartographer tracks deforestation in the tropical rainforests remaining on Earth with the help of satellite imagery and data (above).

Some Famous Environmentalists

Many environmentalists work in the wild and in laboratories without ever making the news. Others have become well-known figures in the movement to protect the planet. Read about some of the famous environmentalists on these pages. Maybe someday your name will be added to the list!

JOHN JAMES AUDUBON
This painter and naturalist, born in 1785, published *Birds of America*, a collection of life-size paintings that recorded the avian heritage of North America.

ERNEST EVERETT JUST
This American scientist pioneered study of ocean environments at the Marine Biological Laboratory in Woods Hole, Massachusetts, in the early twentieth century.

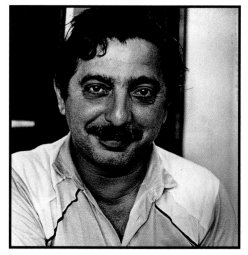

FRANCISCO "CHICO" MENDES
This Brazilian rubber tapper and labor leader was murdered by a group of ranchers in 1988. The *New York Times* said he died for "defending the forest."

ANSEL ADAMS
This photographer's work capturing North America's wild places, much of it published by the Sierra Club, influenced environmentalism in the United States.

DENIS HAYES
"The people heard the cry of the Earth and came to heal her," said Denis Hayes, activist organizer of the first Earth Day in 1970 and chair of Earth Day 2000.

ROBERT REDFORD
This popular American actor has used his fame to promote environmental causes and to draw attention to the need to preserve wild land in the American West.

JOHN CRAIGHEAD
With his twin brother, Frank, this wildlife biologist pioneered ways of using radio collars to track animals electronically.

YVON CHOUINARD
This American outdoorsman founded Patagonia, a company that makes gear from recyclables such as plastic bottles.

VO QUY
This conservationist stars in a Vietnamese TV program that explores the natural world and why it needs to be protected.

JIM DARLING
This marine biologist took whale research to a new level in the 1970s by tracking individual whales and their songs.

CHIEF SEATTLE
He once said, "Man did not weave the web of life; he is merely a strand in it. Whatever he does to the web, he does to himself."

MARJORY STONEMAN DOUGLAS
This writer's 1947 book, *The Everglades: River of Grass,* continues to draw attention to Florida's fragile environmental treasure.

ALBERT GORE JR. AND JANE GOODALL
Before becoming vice president, Gore wrote *Earth in the Balance*. Here he gives a medal to primatologist Goodall.

JACQUES-YVES COUSTEAU
This French pioneer of undersea exploration revealed in his films the mysteries and wonders of the undersea world.

WILLIAM WONG
At age 11 this San Francisco, California, resident won the first Young Eco Inventors contest with a design for a solar car.

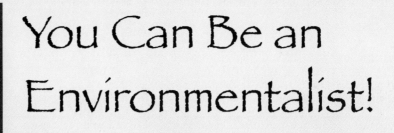

You Can Be an Environmentalist!

Many kids are active members of the environmental movement. Melissa Poe of Nashville, Tennessee, started her work as an environmentalist back in 1991, when she wrote a letter to President George Bush asking him to stop pollution. She didn't get an answer, so Melissa plastered her message across billboards and spoke out on local television stations. Melissa also founded a club called Kids for a Clean Environment, also known as Kids FACE. The club, with a current membership of three hundred thousand worldwide, was established to help kids learn about the world in which they live, to encourage them to help protect nature—and to connect them with other children who share their concerns about global environmental issues. Melissa and her club created a gigantic Kids' Earth Flag to dramatize their concern for the planet. That's a small part of the quilt Melissa's holding at left. The quilt has twenty thousand squares designed and made by kids from countries around the globe, including Japan and Australia. The squares illustrate endangered flowers, trees, and animals. It made its debut in 1995 at Earth Day celebrations in Washington, D.C. In 1997, when she turned eighteen, Melissa stepped down as head of the club but continues to work with Kids FACE as a mentor to other young people. Melissa said, "I've always wanted Kids FACE to be for kids and run by kids. Plus, there's more stuff I'm excited to try—like going to college and maybe even being president one day."

As you read this book, you learned about many different ways to get involved in cleaning up our planet and protecting it for future generations. To find out more about how you can put these ideas into action, turn the page.

Other Sources of Information

U.S. GOVERNMENT ORGANIZATIONS:

National Oceanic and Atmospheric Administration (NOAA)
14th Street and
Constitution Avenue, NW
Room 6013
Washington, DC 20230

NOAA's mission is to describe and predict changes in the earth's environment and to manage wisely the nation's coastal and marine resources.

U.S. Environmental Protection Agency (EPA)
401 M Street, SW
Washington, DC 20460

The mission of the EPA is to protect human health and to safeguard the natural environment.

U.S. Fish and Wildlife Service
1849 C Street, NW, MIB 3012
Washington, DC 20240

This service works to conserve, protect, and enhance fish and wildlife and their habitats.

U.S. ENVIRONMENTAL ORGANIZATIONS:

Center for Environmental Education
881 Alma Real Drive
Pacific Palisades, CA 90272

This group is a clearinghouse for environmental education programs.

Center for Renewable Energy and Sustainable Technology (CREST)
1200 18th Street, NW, #90
Washington, DC 20036

CREST is an education and training group dedicated to renewable energy and energy-efficient technology.

Defenders of Wildlife
1101 14th Street, NW
Suite 1400
Washington, DC 20005

This group works to protect wildlife, particularly endangered species.

Earth Day USA
P.O. Box 470
Peterborough, NH 03458

This organization facilitates regional and local Earth Day celebrations and promotes the public observance of the day on April 22 each year.

The Environmental Careers Organization (ECO)
179 South Street, 5th Floor
Boston, MA 02111

ECO provides information to college students about careers in environmental science and action.

Environmental Defense Fund
257 Park Avenue, South
New York, NY 10010

This organization encourages control of global warming, preservation of wetlands, decreased ozone depletion, and increased recycling.

National Audubon Society
700 Broadway
New York, NY 10003

This group is known for its work championing birds and bird habitat but also focuses on ecosystem conservation and restoration.

Natural Resources Defense Council
40 West 20th Street, 11th Floor
New York, NY 10011

This organization of lawyers and scientists brings legal action to preserve natural resources around the country.

The Nature Conservancy
4245 North Fairfax Drive
Arlington, VA 22203

This group purchases and manages land in order to protect biological diversity.

National Wildlife Federation (NWF)
1400 16th Street, NW
Suite 501
Washington, DC 20036

With several million members, the NWF is the largest conservation organization in the United States.

Sierra Club
730 Polk Street
San Francisco, CA 94109

Founded in 1892, this large conservation group with more than sixty chapters around the country focuses on the protection of biodiversity and wilderness areas.

Wildlife Conservation Society (WCS)

2300 Southern Boulevard
Bronx, NY 10460

Founded in 1895 as the New York Zoological Society, the WCS is head-quartered at the Bronx Zoo in New York City and works to save wildlife and wildlands throughout the world.

INTERNATIONAL ENVIRONMENTAL ORGANIZATIONS:

Caretakers of the Environment International

13422 Stardust Boulevard
Sun City West, AZ 85375

This international network helps students from India to Ireland to the United States work together on environment-related projects.

Friends of the Earth

1025 Vermont Avenue, NW
Suite 300
Washington, DC 20005

This international group focuses on worldwide issues, including global warming, depletion of the ozone layer, and the destruction of rainforests.

World Wildlife Fund (WWF)

1250 24th Street, NW
Washington, DC 20037

Known worldwide by its panda logo, the WWF is dedicated to protecting the world's wildlife and the rich biological diversity we all need to survive. WWF has sponsored more than 2,000 projects in 116 countries.

Conservation International

2501 M Street, NW
Suite 200
Washington, DC 20037

This group's mission is to conserve global biodiversity and to demonstrate that people can live in harmony with the environment.

SELECTED CHILDREN'S ENVIRONMENTAL ORGANIZATIONS:

Children's Alliance for Protection of the Environment (CAPE)

P.O. Box 307
Austin, TX 78767

This global children's network provides information about hands-on projects, from beach cleanup and tree plantings to the preservation of rainforests.

Kids Action Team (KAT)

Rainforest Action Network
221 Pine Street
Suite 500
San Francisco, CA 94104

KAT was created to inspire young people to learn about rainforests and take action to help save them.

Kids for a Clean Environment (Kids FACE)

P.O. Box 158254
Nashville, TN 37215

This is one of the largest children's environmental groups, with 300,000 members worldwide.

Project Wild

707 Conservation Lane
Suite 305
Gaithersburg, MD 20878

This K–12 conservation and environmental education program emphasizes the protection of wildlife.

PHOTO CREDITS